Successful Strategies for Marketing School Levies

by
Glenn T. Graham,
Gordon L. Wise,
and
Duane L. Bachman

Library of Congress Catalog Card Number 90-62019
ISBN 0-87367-310-7
Copyright © 1990 by the Phi Delta Kappa Educational Foundation
Bloomington, Indiana

This fastback is sponsored by the University of Akron Chapter of Phi Delta Kappa, which made a generous contribution toward publication costs.

Table of Contents

Introduction

With a roller-coaster economy and increasing taxpayer resistance — even revolt in some communities — gaining approval of bonds or levies to build or renovate school facilities is no easy task. However, there is a new champion emerging for gaining public support. It's called MARKETING. While the art of marketing is not new, its applications outside the business sector have made significant inroads in the last two decades.

To many, marketing is synonymous with selling. Not so! Selling is getting rid of what you have. *Marketing is having what you can get rid of.* This distinction is not a glib turn of phrase; it is a critical element in developing a successful marketing approach. When a business focuses all its energy on getting rid of what it has — a product, inventory, idea, or service — it typically uses high pressure advertising and spends huge amounts of money to make the market desire the product. But in trying to find a place for it in the market, the business is ignoring the actual needs or desires of those who constitute the market.

By contrast, the modern marketing concept focuses on customers or consumers and takes into consideration their needs, desires, values, and satisfactions. The marketing objective then becomes one of maximizing consumer satisfaction. Whereas selling involves solving the problem of the seller, marketing involves solving the problem of the consumer. It is this latter perspective that public schools can use in their efforts to gain and maintain financial as well as other forms of support from their market — the citizens in the community.

Since 1977, we have been using modern marketing concepts to assist school districts in passing levies and bond issues. Our successes have been impressive. Communities that had repeatedly voted down levies have turned around and passed them by more than 60%. In this fastback we share some of our rich experiences in the hope that others will find applications to their own situations and enjoy the benefits of success.

Modern Marketing Tools

The marketing tools that school districts can use for their financial campaigns include:

1. Identification and analysis of the target market to be served
2. Product development
3. Price development and administration
4. Promotion development and administration
5. Physical distribution
6. Follow-up market analysis

A brief description of each of the tools follows.

Identification and analysis of the target market to be served. Before any product or mix of products can be developed for a market, it is necessary to determine the precise segment of the market to be served and its needs, desires, and expected levels of satisfaction. This requires some type of market research, usually in the form of a survey to answer such questions as:

Who are the members of the market to be served?

What does the market need?

How well are those needs currently being met?

What areas of additional satisfaction can be developed for the market?

For schools these questions translate into identifying the issues critical to the acceptance or rejection of levies and bond issues by voters. Not only must the issues be identified, but their strength or intensity must be assessed. Preconceived notions of the issues, without verification, may lead to campaigns with the wrong focus; and time, money, and energy are expended in fruitless labors.

Product development. For schools the product to be developed is the levy or bond issue. Central to product development is identifying those satisfactions associated with its passage, that is, what voters see as its benefits. Once identified, they should become the focus for the campaign. By the same token, it is important to identify what voters see as dissatisfactions, what will they lose if it passes. These, too, must be addressed, as positively as possible, in the campaign. We will have more to say about this later. Identifying the satisfactions and dissatisfactions is another important function of the market survey.

Development of a price strategy. For a school levy or bond issue the price will be reflected in the form of a tax or millage increase. How much will voters be willing to sacrifice (pay) in order to gain the satisfactions resulting from passage of the levy or bond issue? Again the market survey can be used to determine the millage rate that would be acceptable.

Development of a promotional strategy. Once the needs, desires, and expected satisfactions are determined, they become the focus for all promotional materials, presentations, and other activities for the campaign. Promotion includes all forms of media and nonmedia advertising, public presentations, and public relations activities. Subsequent sections of this fastback will address promotional strategies in detail.

Development of a physical distribution strategy. This element of a school finance campaign concerns how the benefits from a levy or bond issue will be allocated or distributed. The decision regarding the location of a new school is an example of physical distribution strategy. The political sensitivity of decisions of this nature can be used in designing the campaign strategy; for example, concentrating campaign promotion activities in the targeted area.

Follow-up research activities. Follow-up research is necessary to learn what worked and what did not, which campaign elements were successful and which were not. This information will be useful when planning future campaigns. It is important that this assessment be made promptly after the campaign is over while the details are fresh in the minds of those who conducted the campaign.

Conducting the Market Analysis

Planning for an effective market analysis must start early — eight months to a year prior to the election, with the market survey conducted about six months prior to the election. Factors to be considered in the market analysis include:

- Funding the cost of the analysis
- Development of a market survey instrument
- Selection of a sample to be surveyed
- Personnel to conduct and analyze the survey
- Projection of the voting outcome
- Development of a market plan

Following is a discussion on each of these factors.

Funding the Market Survey

Costs for a market analysis can vary widely depending on whether it is done primarily with volunteers or by employing professional consultants. The range can run from $1,000 (using all volunteers) to more than $10,000 (using professional consultants), but in general a school district should budget about $3,000 to $6,000.

In many states it is legal for school board funds to be used to finance the community survey, but it may be illegal to use board funds to develop a market plan based on the survey results or to finance the campaign itself. In a later section we will discuss methods for soliciting outside funding.

Developing the Survey Instrument

In developing the survey instrument, the first decision is whether to use door-to-door personal interviews, phone surveys, or mail surveys. Many people get annoyed by one more phone call that interrupts what they are doing at the moment. The last thing you want to do in a financial campaign is antagonize the voters. Mail surveys tend to get responses from the extremes — those most positive and those most negative. In general, these are not the people who will determine the outcome of an election.

From our experience the best results come from personal interviews. You are likely to get more honest answers in a face-to-face interview. And interviewers can pick up nuances in the responses that a mail survey would not reveal. If you can recruit volunteers or if you can afford to hire a consulting firm, the personal interview is the best procedure for obtaining the information on which to build a successful campaign.

In most communities there will be about one-third of the voters who will vote in favor of school levies no matter what. There is another third who will steadfastly vote against the schools. Dynamite wouldn't move them to change their minds! However, it is approximately the one-third in the middle who actually will determine whether the levy passes or fails. But you probably won't hear from them in a mail survey. In designing a successful campaign, you will need to know the issues that will sway the middle to vote yes.

Once the type of survey procedure has been selected, the items to be included in the survey must be drafted. How do you decide what to ask? Consider using focus groups, three or four groups of about 10 to 12 people each who represent a cross-section of the community (politicians, teachers, students, parents, administrators, civil servants, professionals, positive people, negative people). Invite people who are articulate and have ideas. Explain to each group that you are concerned with how the community feels about the bond or levy. Ask the group what they see as the issues or concerns in the community. The notes from these discussions will provide the basis for your survey questions.

The space limitations of this fastback do not allow detailed directions for writing survey items, but here are some suggestions we find useful.

1. Answers to questions should be brief. The easiest way to do this is to develop questions that ask the respondents to choose from a list of alternatives rather than compose their own answer. Examples include:

   a. attitudinal statements to which the respondents reply "strongly agree," "agree," "undecided," "disagree," and "strongly disagree."

   b. giving a grade, A, B C, D, or F for different school programs, for example.

   c. multiple-choice items whereby persons choose the response that best represents their opinion or attitude.

   d. rating a list of issues as "very important," "somewhat important," or "not important." (This type of question is especially helpful in determining factors that would cause people to vote for or against the bond or levy.)

   e. ranking items whereby respondents pick their top two or three and bottom two or three choices from a list. (These types of items are very helpful in isolating the major issues or nonissues.

2. Keep the time required to respond to the survey as short as possible. Using the types of items described in #1 above will help to keep the response time brief. For interviews, limit the number of questions so that it does not take more than about 15 minutes. If you conduct a phone or mail survey, keep it to about 10 minutes. You will get fewer refusals.

3. Respondents should remain anonymous. When introducing the survey, tell the respondents you will not use their name – do not even ask it. Tell them you want them to answer in terms of how they feel, not how they are supposed to feel. Tell them there are no right or wrong answers – just honest answers.

4. Avoid asking questions that may be perceived as personally threatening or an invasion of one's privacy. For example, asking one's income or grades in school might cause some people to stop the interview. Where a response to a question is crucial to the survey, give respondents some options. Instead of asking directly, "How will you vote on the levy?" ask them which of the following choices expresses their feeling: "I'd certainly vote for it," "I'd almost certainly vote for it," "I'd probably vote for it," "I'm uncertain how I'd vote," "I'd probably vote against it," "I'd almost certainly vote against it," "I'd certainly vote against it." Later we'll show how to use this question to project the voting outcome.

5. Try out the survey instrument in advance. Never administer an untested survey. In every market survey instrument we have developed, we have found it necessary to revise after a tryout. Select about 10 to 12 people from your community and administer the survey to them. If it is to be an interview, read them the questions in person. If it is to be a phone survey, call them on the phone. Record the time it takes to conduct the survey. When you have finished, go over each item. Check for ambiguities, clarity, terminology, biases, ease of response, appropriateness of choices, unnecessary questions, and omitted areas.

6. When possible, give the survey responses numerical values for easy computer entry. For example, if the item has a choice of five responses – "Strongly Agree," "Agree," "Undecided," "Disagree," or "Strongly Disagree" – assign a number value of 1 to 5 for each choice. The interviewer records the number of the respondent's choices on the survey form, thus making it easy for the person doing data entry for later computer analysis. This will save considerable time.

7. Publicize the survey. Starting about a week before the survey begins, announce in the local newspaper and on local radio and TV stations that you are conducting the survey to determine the attitudes of the community toward the bond or levy. Stress the importance of their cooperation, honesty of response, and assurance of anonymity. State that the names of the interviewers have been filed with the local police, and that anyone should call if uneasy when someone comes to the door. Provide the dates and times of the interviews in the announcement. Any day of the week is appropriate, but don't start before 10:00 a.m. and on Sundays before 1:00 p.m.; finish no later than 9:00 p.m. Furnish your interviewers with a badge and/or photo ID to be shown when arriving at a household.

8. Try to anticipate cataclysmic events. A week before we were to conduct our first school market survey, we found out that, as a result of reassessment, property taxes were to increase about 15% and that people would not be getting their tax statements until after the survey. Fortunately, we were able to delay the survey and incorporate questions to test the effects of the property reassessments. In another case, we had the largest employer in the community go out of business. Events of this nature can have a dramatic effect on people's attitudes and how they respond to the survey. Check with the treasurer, auditor, or Chamber of Commerce about local conditions before completing the construction of your survey and continue to monitor conditions during the campaign. In analyses that we have done, the impact of cataclysmic events has been immediate but soon starts to diminish. By six weeks the effects have just about disappeared.

Selecting the Sample

Whom to survey is a crucial question. The selection of a sample needs to be done carefully and without bias. It is beyond the scope of this fastback to detail the statistical procedures for determining size of sample and margin of error. Typically you'll need a sample of 300 to 400 people to give you a margin of error of about plus or minus

5%. In other words, with a sample of this size, if 65% say "yes" to a question, then in the total population of the community the number who would say "yes" would fall somewhere between 60% to 70%.

To set up a sample, start by getting the results of the most recent elections in which a school finance issue appeared. Look at the voter turnout in each precinct or ward and determine its percentage of the total vote. For example, if 4,000 total votes were cast in the past election and precinct 37 cast 400 votes, then it had 10% of the vote. Let's say you decided to have a sample of 300 people surveyed. Then 10% of your sample or 30 people would come from precinct 37. Repeat this process for every precinct.

Next, get a community map that delineates the precincts. For each precinct list the names of all the streets and number them. For example, if precinct 37 had 16 streets, the names would be written down and numbered from 1 to 16. Get a table of random numbers (found in the back of most statistics textbooks) and randomly select the streets needed. Each time a number occurs you will pick that many people from that street. Let's say that Ash Street is number 6 on the list of streets in precinct 37. If out of the 30 numbers selected between 1 and 16 the number 6 occurs four times, then four households will be selected from Ash Street with one person per household being interviewed. Note that a household also could be an apartment unit.

Using these procedures gives you the number of households but not the specific household. Instruct your interviewers: "Select four houses from Ash Street. If you are refused at one household, go to the next house. Try to cover the whole street, not just a small section." While this whole process may sound cumbersome, with a little practice it becomes quite easy. Adhering strictly to the sampling procedure is essential in order to avoid sample bias and to make the survey statistically reliable.

When interviewers visit a household, they should speak with one person who is of voting age. It is not necessary that this person be a registered voter. In fact, it is useful to have unregistered people in your sample in order to get the views of this segment of the population. And remember, even if unregistered at the time of the interview, the person may become registered before the election.

Personnel to Conduct and Analyze the Survey

Under ideal circumstances a market survey should be conducted by experienced interviewers. If using volunteers, they will need some training. Here are a few tips for interviewers:

1. Go to neighborhoods where you are not known. Do not interview friends, relatives, or acquaintances.
2. Read through the survey questions several times until you are thoroughly familiar with them. Do a few practice interviews before starting with the real ones.
3. Do not discuss the results of your interviews with anyone except those analyzing the results. If word gets out about what was said or who said it, the credibility of the survey is compromised.
4. Be courteous. The respondents will view you as an extension of the schools. Your actions could possibly affect how someone will vote.
5. Do not express agreement or disagreement with the respondent's answers. Assure them there are no right or wrong answers; your only function is to record their answers.
6. Do not campaign. If a respondent is negative, so be it. Do not try to change his mind during the interview. The campaign comes later.
7. Avoid nonverbal and body language cues. Do not smile when they say something you like and frown when they say something you don't. Be pleasant and noncommittal.
8. If someone refuses to be interviewed, be gracious and do not plead. Thank them and leave. If someone is hesitant, explain the importance of the survey and assure their anonymity. If

suspicious, suggest they call the police to verify your legitimacy.

9. Keep a count of the number of refusals. These may be indicative of a negative attitude toward the bond or levy.

10. Be sure to record the demographic data on your sample. Those who analyze the survey data not only want to tabulate the percentage of responses to each question but also need to be able to cross-tabulate answers by demographics: Do men and women respond differently? Are there differences depending on age? Do registered voters differ from those unregistered? Are there differences between high and low income neighborhoods?

Projecting the Voting Outcome

Earlier we gave an example of a how to phrase a question for asking people how they would vote on a school levy or bond. Such a question can be used to make a conservative estimate of the voting outcome were the vote held at the time of the survey. Remember, people have responded to the survey without yet having been exposed to campaign promotion. To estimate the vote, take:

90% of those responding "certainly vote for"
60% of those responding "almost certainly vote for"
30% of those responding "probably vote for"
10% of those responding "uncertain"

Divide the sum of these by the total number of surveys and you have the projected estimate for a "yes" vote. In our experiences, good marketing campaigns can add 10% to 20% to the projection. So, if you project more than 40%, you have a good chance of winning.

Developing the Marketing Plan

The survey analysis should provide the basis for developing the marketing plan. It should answer such questions as:

What will be done (objectives)?
How will it be done (strategies and tactics)?
By whom will it be done (organization, personnel)?
When will it be done (timetable)?
What will it cost (budget)?

The remainder of this fastback will help you put this plan together.

Financing the Campaign

The most critical element for success in any campaign is *personal, one-on-one contact and interaction*. Any costs that support and advance the quantity and quality of personal contact deserve the highest priority when developing the campaign budget.

The first budget consideration should be the printing costs for brochures and other forms of printed material that campaign workers can use as they make their contacts with voters. Producing a simple but attractive brochure is the single best investment that can be made in a campaign. After the printing costs for a brochure, the next most important budget expenditure is for a video or slide/tape that can be used to supplement the brochure when making group presentations. Details for producing the brochure and video or slide/tape presentations will be discussed later.

Media advertising is a part of most campaigns. This is the biggest variable in campaign costs and will depend on the size of the community, the circulation of newspapers, and audience penetration of radio and TV stations. In our opinion, dollars spent on media advertising are "icing on the cake." Certainly there is value in reaching voters via the mass media; however, it is no substitute for persistent and direct personal contact. Many examples exist of successes with little or no media advertising support, but there are very few examples of success where little or no personal contact was used.

As more school districts face difficulty getting voter approval of levies or bond issues, they increasingly are turning to professional consultants to help with their campaigns. Situations that would favor use of outside consultants are:

1. Several failed attempts at gaining voter approval, particularly if defeats have been by wide margins;
2. Approval of a particularly large financial issue, one much larger than has been attempted in the past or one that is trying something entirely new, such as attempting to gain approval of a local income tax where only property tax has been used in the past;
3. A school consolidation or merger, a severe alteration in the social, political, or economic climate in the community, or a sudden spurt in student enrollment.

Great care should be taken in selecting consultants. Obtain documentation of past experience before hiring a consultant. While the total costs can range greatly; a reasonable estimate would be from a minimum of $2,500 to a maximum of $20,000.

Outside Funding and Involvement

If a bond issue or levy campaign is to be successful, outside funding and involvement is imperative. In many states campaigns cannot be funded with school monies. As a result, it is common practice to ask local business and industry to contribute money and in-kind services for the campaign.

The local Chamber of Commerce is one of the first and earliest contacts to be made. Its support is invaluable, not only financially but also in providing campaign leadership and design. Many of the members are highly visible and respected in the community, and their endorsement can gain positive votes. Their expertise in organization and advertising and their spirit of community involvement are resources waiting to be tapped. In addition to the Chamber of Commerce, other agencies should be contacted, including service clubs and fraternal organizations, many of which have a stated mission of serving the needs of community youth.

Additional support and influence for a successful campaign might come from the health service professions. We have received voluntary participation from medical professionals, who raised sufficient funds to pay for several major ads and even signed the ad, urging support for the school bond issue.

Also in the mainstream of a community's leadership structure are presidents and CEOs of local industries. Even though their numbers are small, they have a significant impact on community issues. When they collectively endorse the campaign by allowing their signatures to be used on a newspaper advertisement, voters are likely to be impressed. In addition, these people may be effectively used as authors (or signers) of supportive letters sent to the editorial page of a newspaper.

Organizing the Campaign

One of the common shortcomings of campaigns is failure to allow sufficient time for planning and organization. In our experience the most successful campaigns are those in which the complete organization is in place about six months prior to the election. The campaign itself will be relatively short — about two to three weeks prior to the election — but the planning and development tasks must be completed well before the onset of the campaign and will take the bulk of the time.

Pre-Campaign Development and Control

The blueprint for the campaign should evolve from the market analysis or other methods of assessing community attitudes. The positive issues that may encourage a "yes" vote must be built into the campaign design and into all promotional plans. Likewise, any negative issues identified must be addressed in planning the campaign. Avoiding discussion of negative issues on the assumption that you can divert voters from thinking about such matters is misguided thinking. A genuine negative issue will surface in a "Letter to the Editor" if it has not already seen the light of day through other informal channels. Stonewalling a negative issue will likely hurt your campaign by undermining your credibility ("They have something to hide. They are not telling us all of the story," etc.).

Organizational Structure of the Campaign

In this section we outline the structure of a successful campaign organization and describe the roles of different personnel in the structure.

Steering Committee. This committee provides the overall direction for the campaign. Membership on this committee should include, but not be limited to, the following:

Campaign chair(s);

Campaign treasurer;

Campaign consultant (optional);

Representatives from the Chamber of Commerce, board of education, school administration, teachers and staff, students, and parents; and

Chairs of each division (residential, manufacturing, professional, special events).

Other members may be added to the steering committee. In the most successful campaigns we have experienced, there was a pastor on the steering committee, who enlisted the support of the clergy in the community. The opportunity to address members of local congregations through church bulletins, newsletters, and even through sermons should not be overlooked.

Campaign chair. This extremely important position must be filled by a person who is dedicated, competent, highly visible in the community, and who has a schedule flexible enough to allow participation in the full range of leadership activities required for the campaign. If there are co-chairs, at least one should be female. The day-to-day direction of the campaign rests with the chair. All campaign-related announcements and information should come through the chair.

Primary areas of involvement include recruitment and training of all volunteer workers; coordinating volunteer activities; development of campaign theme and slogans; development of campaign advertising plan; development of campaign brochure; approval of all advertising copy to be used in the media; scheduling and placement of all advertising; scheduling and coordination of all promotional activities, such as news releases and feature stories; and chairing the steering committee.

Campaign treasurer. The responsibilities of this position are to record all financial transactions, approve all expenditures (after conferring with the campaign chair), sign checks for campaign expenses, and complete all reports and forms required by state election laws.

Campaign consultant (optional). The consultant serves in an advisory capacity to the campaign chair but should be able to function in a variety of roles behind the scenes as needed. Sometimes there is concern that the use of an outside consultant introduces a "foreign" flavor that could alienate both campaign workers and voters. From our experience, if the consultant is knowledgeable, competent, and has good interpersonal skills, then he or she will be appreciated for the expertise and specialized leadership provided.

Chair of the Residential Division. It is the responsibility of the Residential Division to identify the positive voters, to distribute campaign materials to them, and to get their commitment to vote. The chair of this division selects leaders for each of the wards or townships in the community. Each ward and township leader then selects coordinators for each precinct or neighborhood, and each of these selects a series of block captains. Each of the captains in turn is responsible for recruiting and directing a group of two to five volunteers.

The Residential Division chair oversees a key component of the campaign organization, which is a systematic effort to reach into every neighborhood within the school district. To accomplish this, a large number of volunteers (perhaps several hundred) is needed. Recruiting, training, and motivating this group is a first priority of the campaign leadership.

Chair of the Manufacturing Division. This division works with two groups of voters and potential vote influencers — manufacturing employers and employees. Responsibilities can be shared by two persons. For the manufacturing employers the person should be a prominent and respected industrialist whose responsibilities include obtaining endorsements and support from other industry leaders, appearing in newspaper and radio ads, and writing letters to the editor. For the manufacturing employees, the person should be a respected union member who can effectively communicate to organized labor groups the importance of supporting the public schools. Responsibilities include coordinating promotional activities within each unionized factory or facility and gaining the union's endorsement of the levy (at least informally).

Chair of the Business/Professional Division. The chair of this division works to obtain the endorsement and support of business leaders and members of the professional community.

Chair of the Special Events and Promotions Division. This person is responsible for special promotional activities, such as parades, celebrity gatherings, and other community events.

Targeting and Registering Positive Voters

Perhaps the greatest value of a market analysis is in determining which groups of voters to target in the campaign. In the market analyses we have conducted, we have found that of those who were not registered to vote, usually more than 70% percent had a negative attitude toward the levy or bond issue. A mass voter registration campaign to get this group registered would likely result in the defeat of the levy. Therefore we recommend that any voter registration campaign be targeted at registering positive voters.

In planning a selective voter registration campaign to reach unregistered but potentially positive voters, allow enough lead time (a minimum of four months) before the election for training volunteers to carry out the assignment. Providing training to voter registration volunteers ensures a consistent approach and gives them an opportunity to discuss various strategies.

One of the strategies we have found successful is "packaging" of residences in the school district. Lists of about ten households are compiled and assigned to the volunteer as his "territory." In contrast to market survey volunteers, we recommend that volunteers for voter registration work in their own neighborhoods.

As the volunteers contact each household on their list, they should unobtrusively bring up the topic of the upcoming levy or bond issue with the intent of determining how each eligible adult resident might vote. A casual comment such as, "I will be the neighborhood volunteer this fall when the levy/bond issue campaign is conducted. Are there any questions you would like to ask or any information I can get for you?" In this way volunteers can usually identify positive and negative voters without getting involved in any direct campaigning or arguing with the resident. Once volunteers determine that a respondent is positive, they can ask if the resident is registered and, if not, provide information about how to register to vote. In many areas volunteers can be deputized and register people on the spot.

From the neighborhood contacts, the volunteer should compile a list of positive, registered voters including name, address, and precinct. This list is then used in a variety of ways (discussed in subsequent sections) during the campaign and on election day to ensure the best possible turnout of positive voters.

Finding Voters Who Don't Pay Property Taxes

A substantial segment of voters in many communities are renters who pay rent in the form of a fixed proportion of their income. They live in apartment complexes, and many of them are not registered. Because they pay rent based on their income, they are not directly affected by a property tax increase. You can say to them, "You can support the schools and kids, and it will not cost you a dime to do so."

In approaching this significant voter segment, the ideal arrangement is to have a two-person team consisting of a member of the campaign organization and a neighborhood voter registration volunteer, who ideally is a resident of the apartment complex. People tend to feel more comfortable talking to this team, and it provides an opportunity to explain the need for the levy or bond issue. They tend to be cooperative and are relatively easy to register if the procedure is explained. To be able to assist others at no cost to themselves is a combination that few will turn down. Turning out this voter segment on election day can make the difference in a close election.

Registering Students and Military Personnel

Another significant group that should be not overlooked in voter registration campaigns are students and military personnel — both of whom are grossly underrepresented on voting rolls. Many students reach voting age in their senior year of high school and should be contacted. College students and military personnel who are away from home should be identified by the campaign committee and sent registration materials. In a cover letter, indicate that absentee ballots can be requested. Enclose an application for an absentee ballot.

Reaching young voters is an ideal assignment for your student volunteer committee. Try to recruit these volunteers from the past five years' graduating classes. Contact from peers is likely to result in more voter registrations and a positive response to the levy on election day.

Student committee members should follow up just prior to or on election day to remind newly registered students to go the polls. When sending campaign materials to college students and military personnel, include a reminder to send in their absentee ballots.

Tracking Positive Voters

From the lists of positive, registered voters made by the neighborhood volunteers, a master list should be compiled, broken down by precinct, and then alphabetized with address and telephone number for each voter. During the days just prior to or on election day, all people on the master list of positive voters should receive a telephone call from their neighborhood volunteer urging them to vote.

In many communities on election day, a list of registered voters is posted outside the polls. Campaign workers can check off names as people come to vote. Then using their alphabetized lists of positive voters, they can see who has not yet voted and call them. Campaign workers should be prepared to offer transportation or even short-term baby-sitting service if necessary. In our experience, it is possible to add a substantial number of positive votes in this way.

It does require careful organization and additional hours of volunteer effort, but the payoff can be great.

Launching the Campaign

Early in the planning stage, a name and theme should be selected for the levy campaign. It helps if the name can be made into an acronym. For example, in the campaign planned for Piqua, Ohio, the organization was known as Piqua's Active School Supporters or PASS. The fact that the campaign was to be conducted in the fall during football season made the acronym particularly appropriate. More meaningful, however, was the identification of the organization's intentions.

Along with a name is the need for a theme, which becomes the rallying cry for all that is done in behalf of the campaign. Some of the themes we have used are: "This Is the Year," "It's Time to Take a Stand," and "It's Up to Us." In one community, which had had an earlier unsuccessful campaign, we used, "It's Still Up to Us."

Launching the campaign should be treated as a news event that is tied to the opening of the campaign headquarters or a kick-off dinner or luncheon for the campaign officials and all the volunteers. Provide a press release to the media several days in advance of these events and request that it be carried as local news. It is useful to follow up on the press releases with a personal call. By making the kick-off activities a news event, the major issues of the campaign can be identified and addressed in a favorable setting.

Opening the campaign headquarters might involve a ribbon-cutting ceremony or the unveiling of a sign that identifies the headquarters. This also could be the occasion for introducing the campaign leadership. If the headquarters space has been donated, this is an opportunity to recognize and thank the benefactor. Also, a campaign kick-off typically involves a luncheon or banquet attended by the steering committee and, if possible, all the campaign volunteers. Paying for the meal out of campaign funds may have a negative impact on the voters. Alternatives are getting the meal donated, making it a pot-luck affair, or charging for the meal.

If possible, a guest speaker — one without a vested interest in the campaign — should be invited to the kick-off activities to speak on issues related to the campaign. For example, in one campaign with which we were associated, the market survey identified a major concern in the community to be economic issues. Therefore, the speaker invited for the kick-off banquet was an economist from a regional university. He was able to address the economic impact schools have on a community by attracting industry, jobs, and new residents and by making current residents want to remain in the community. If the speaker and campaign leadership are available for interviews by the local media, it is possible for the campaign message to reach thousands of voters without expending any precious promotional dollars.

Specific Campaign Strategies

There are many ways to conduct a levy or bond issue campaign. We share here some we have used successfully and invite others to use or adapt them for their own campaigns.

Testimonials

Prominent people in the community — clergy, doctors, dentists, business and civic leaders — can be very helpful to the campaign by providing testimonials that can be used in the media advertising program. All it takes is asking them. Although accustomed to writing and speaking, these are very busy people, so many may be amenable to lending their name to a testimonial that is ghostwritten, as long as they have the right to approve the copy. When this can be arranged, in essence it gives the campaign leaders an opportunity to speak through the mouths of people who command respect in the community and to address the issues they wish to have addressed.

One of the best kinds of ads is what we call the "I've Changed My Mind" testimonial. This is from someone who has been negative about the levy in the past but realizes now how important it is for the schools and the community. Voters who are on the fence can identify with someone who has the courage to say publicly, "I changed my mind, and I now support the school levy." And remember that each time you convert a negative voter to a positive voter, you have changed two votes — by subtracting one from the negative column and adding one to the positive column.

What's It Going to Cost?

There is a price attached to passage of a levy or bond issue — usually in the form of a tax increase. Voters tend to overestimate what they will have to pay, which, of course, only serves to heighten their resistance. To counteract this resistance, it is important to provide some perspective about tax increases.

We have found an effective tool to be a tax table that compares the increase in property taxes with the present level of taxes paid, rather than comparing it to the current market value. This table should be simple to interpret but include enough detail so voters will be able to determine the actual tax increase for a wide range of amounts. We also recommended that the tax increase be broken down into costs per day. In this way the costs seem relatively small when compared with other daily expenditures. In constructing such a table, accuracy is extremely important. Input from the county auditor or treasurer will be needed to ensure accuracy.

Such a table can be used in different components of the campaign program. Certainly it should be included in any brochure developed for campaign use as well as in media advertising, with an appropriate concluding message, such as: "For such a reasonable price, how can we afford to say no to our schools?"

Slide-Tape or Video Presentation

An effective audiovisual presentation can be a major tool for communicating the campaign issues. It can be used to present a consistent message to the community and serve as a virtual "speakers bureau" for the campaign committee.

The presentation should be produced well in advance of the campaign. Preparing the slides or videotaping the footage plus writing and editing the narrative is a time-consuming process. It undoubtedly will require the technical assistance of a media specialist. The presentation should address all the issues that were identified in the earlier market survey and analysis.

Once the presentation has been developed, it should be shown first to campaign chairs and volunteers to ensure they have a full understanding of its contents, to answer any questions they may have, and to correct any technical errors. With formal approval by the campaign committee, the appropriate community groups should be made aware of its availability.

A Campaign Song

A campaign song is a good project for students working in the campaign. It serves as a creative activity for them that is fun and involves them in a tangible way in promoting the campaign. Some adult should check the lyrics for tastefulness. Young people do get carried away at times. The song could be recorded by the school choir and used as background for TV or radio ads. Additional opportunities to sing the song may come if students are asked to present programs during community activities. Be sure to obtain publisher approval if adapting a song that is still under copyright.

Question of the Day

Well before the campaign begins, approach newspapers and radio stations to see if they would, without cost, publish or announce as a public service a question and answer to be provided by the campaign committee for each day of the campaign. If they agree, set up a schedule so that the same question is used on the radio and the newspaper on the same day. The schedule could be structured so that critical questions could be repeated several times during the campaign.

Campaign Brochure

A good brochure should be the centerpiece of your campaign strategy. It must be planned and produced well in advance and be ready for distribution about three weeks before the election. The brochure should be attractive but not so slick that voters will think it an extravagant use of taxpayers' money — even when it is not. The text should be easy to read and brief enough so that it can be perused in five to seven minutes. It might include the tax table mentioned earlier and possibly a Q & A section that anticipates the kinds of questions that will arise.

Radio and TV Call-In Programs

Call-in programs on local radio stations and community cable television are other outlets for getting across the campaign message. By the kinds of questions asked, these programs also can provide a reading on community attitudes. The programs will need to be staffed by a panel that is well informed about the campaign issues, including representatives of the board of education, campaign leadership, and school administration. Also consider including teachers, students, and parents, who will add a different perspective. If there is a campaign song, use it to introduce and close the program. The TV station might agree to show the campaign videotape at some point during the program.

To ensure that important issues are addressed, arrange to have designated persons call in with specific questions, for which the panel will be prepared in advance to answer. If possible, reserve the right to screen questions that are irrelevant or inappropriate. It is best to schedule call-in programs toward the end of the campaign when specific issues need to be clarified or refuted.

Newspaper Coverage

The local newspaper offers several avenues for carrying the campaign message. Consider using the following:

General coverage. Most newspapers cover school district news on a regular basis. Some even assign a reporter full time to cover the schools. If the school district previously has established good relationships with the education reporter and/or the editor, then the newspaper is likely to be cooperative in covering general campaign news.

Letters to the editor. During the course of the campaign, there should be a sequence of letters to the editor from different constituencies that address key questions and emphasize the benefits that the levy or bond issue will provide. Some of these will come unsolicited, but do not wait for them. Designate respected persons in the community to send letters to the editor. Of course, there will likely be negative letters from those opposing the levy. Certain individuals on the campaign committee should be prepared to respond to negative letters immediately, especially when they contain false or erroneous information.

Editorial endorsement. If you can obtain it, editorial endorsement of the levy or bond issue can be a powerful weapon in the campaign. By providing detailed information about school finances and other issues related to the levy, the editor will have the material needed for writing an editorial endorsement.

School page. In many communities, the newspaper has a section devoted to student activities and student opinion. This presents an excellent opportunity for students to express their views about the campaign issues. And they can be very persuasive when it comes to extolling the benefits they will derive from the levy passage.

Question of the day. Mentioned earlier, this feature in a newspaper keeps the issues before the public on a regular basis during the campaign.

Paid advertising. Post-election surveys have shown that paid advertising in newspapers is effective in influencing voters. A common type of paid advertising is an endorsement from business and civic leaders in the community. Another type is one that lays out the economic benefits for the community. Another approach is to ask businesses to include a "slug" in their own ads near election time; for example, "Vote yes for our school's future."

Radio and TV Coverage

Like newspapers, local radio and public-access TV stations can be used to good advantage for the levy campaign. Call-in programs and "Question of the day" formats are possibilities. Or if the school district has a weekly program, the time can be devoted to discussion of various campaign issues. Other possibilities are:

Special programming. Local radio and TV stations may be willing to carry special programs that have been prepared in advance on audio or videotape. One program might introduce the campaign leadership to the community. Another might discuss the vital issues in the campaign. Still another might focus solely on economic issues.

Public service announcements. Many cable television operations have a "weather screen" channel, which in addition to reporting the weather includes other short messages on the screen. The campaign committee should investigate to see if the TV station would consider running a campaign message at no cost as a public service announcement.

Paid advertising. Buying TV time is expensive. If a decision is made to use it, be sure that the ad is professional quality in terms of graphics, sound, and narration. The ad copy should highlight the issues identified in any earlier market analysis. If there is a campaign song, it might be used as a lead-in or conclusion for the ad.

Town Hall Meetings

A town hall type of meeting provides an open forum for anyone in the community to ask questions about the levy or bond issue. Members of the board of education, school administration, and the campaign committee should be on hand to answer questions, to reaffirm the positive benefits to be derived from the levy, or to refute misinformation that has been circulated. Such a meeting is a good defensive measure to neutralize any "we weren't given all the facts" criticism. As with call-in programs, it is useful to have "plants" ask questions that the campaign committee wants to address publicly. Be sure to invite the media to cover the meeting. Their reporting of the meeting will reach those who were not in attendance.

A School Tour and Model Display

We have found that those who have recently been inside a school building are more likely to be positive voters. A good way to get voters into the school is to give them an opportunity to see a model of the proposed new facility or school renovation project, which the bond issue will fund. In other words, let them see what they will be paying for. The school architects are usually willing to construct the model since their contract depends on the passage of the bond issue. Also request that they prepare a floor plan that shows the number and size of rooms, activity areas, science labs, and gymnasium.

Combine the showing of the model and floor plans with a tour of the building that features different aspects of the school's programs and displays of students' work. Conclude the tour with a showing of the campaign videotape and handing out campaign literature. Involve parent organizations and students in publicizing the model display and school tour. Students also can serve as tour guides.

Other Campaign Activities — Take Your Pick

The following campaign activities have been used successfully in some school districts with which we have worked. Some are small-scale, others require considerable planning and coordination. We offer them as options that might work for you.

Letters to employees. Consider approaching local businesses to see if they would be willing to send a letter to their employees, which discusses the merits of the levy or bond issue and how it will likely affect the local economy and their specific business and encourages employees to vote yes. A variation on this is to request permission to place a campaign poster on the company's bulletin boards. These approaches may not be appropriate if the business has had a history of labor problems and employee morale is low.

Windshield project. A fun way of involving students in a campaign is to ask service station operators to allow students to wash the windshields of customers free. They conclude by giving the driver a card that says, "We are pleased to clean your windshield. We hope you can see your way *clear* to vote YES on _____." The pun will win a smile and perhaps even a vote.

Statement stuffers. Banks and utility companies often include stuffers on a variety of topics in their monthly statements as a public service. Inquire to see if they will include a stuffer on your upcoming levy or bond issue election. The stuffer should be prepared well in advance and must be designed to fit into the size of envelope used by the bank or utility.

Menugram. Many schools distribute a weekly lunch menu, which students take home and post prominently on the refrigerator door. In many homes it is the most frequently referred to piece of literature that the school publishes. Reserve space on the menugram to place a brief message about the levy campaign that urges parents to vote YES on election day.

Lapel badges. A distinctive lapel badge or pin carrying the campaign logo or slogan can be worn by campaign workers as they make their rounds in the neighborhoods. Many companies make these pins with only a short lead time. Ordering in large quantities keeps the unit cost low.

Athletic Events. Campaign information or inserts can be included in the printed programs for athletic events. Many schools now have electronic scoreboards that can carry messages as well as the team scores. Use this technology to present a brief campaign message to a large audience. Another approach is to have campaign workers pass out brochures as people come through the gates at the game.

Table tents. Seek permission from businesses and public buildings that have a lot of in-and-out traffic to set up a table tent to display campaign materials. Remember to assign someone on the campaign committee to keep the tables stocked with materials.

Let's have a parade. If the time of the year is appropriate, consider holding a parade on the Saturday before the election. A parade might include the high school band, drill teams, and student groups with banners who pass out campaign brochures to people along the parade route. The parade could conclude downtown with brief remarks from campaign chairs and others who can give one last push to convince people to come out and vote for the levy or bond issue.

Special Roles in the Campaign

Various groups in the school community have special roles to play in planning and conducting a successful campaign. They include the board of education, the superintendent, the administrative team, teachers and classified personnel, students, and the architects. In this section we discuss the roles of each of these groups.

The Board of Education

The board's first responsibility is to ensure that the decision to initiate a levy or bond issue is made early enough to meet the requirements of the law and to plan an effective campaign. Failure to provide enough lead time could even be construed by voters as a lack of vision on the part of the board. The chances of the levy passing are much greater if the decision of the board to place the levy on the ballot is unanimous. A split vote by the board can present serious obstacles when planning a campaign.

The board should consider every campaign as one that belongs to the people. With the advice of staff, the board should appoint the campaign committee and give it wide latitude in organizing and implementing the campaign. However, the board should reserve the right to approve all campaign materials that go to the public. This ensures that nothing goes out that is in conflict with existing board policy. Once the committee is appointed, the board should recognize its official status with a public announcement.

Board members can and should be active during the campaign, but not in highly visible roles. When board members appear to be running the whole show, voters might consider it as an indication of insufficient interest or commitment on the part of the general community. Roles board members can play include serving as one of several speakers available to community groups, participating on a panel for town hall meetings and call-in programs, and writing a message of support in the district newsletter.

The Superintendent of Schools

The initial responsibility of the superintendent is to accumulate all the information the board needs in deciding to place a levy or bond issue on the ballot. This preliminary work, involving property assessments, tax rates, building costs, community demographics, and many other matters, is essential for sound decision making.

After the decision is made to place the issue on the ballot, the superintendent's role may change. In many campaigns, the superintendent maintains a high profile and is perceived to be the person who runs the campaign committee. Other superintendents prefer to maintain a low profile but continue to exert their leadership behind the scenes. The superintendent may be a member of the campaign committee but should not have veto power. The committee should understand that the only time the superintendent will interfere with the decision-making process is if it takes action that contradicts official board policy.

The Administrative Team

The administrative team should be involved initially in compiling information for the superintendent to forward to the board of education. Their knowledge of the community and the schools is essential in developing the package to be presented to the voters.

Some members of the administrative team should be represented on the campaign committee, and provision should be made to release them from some duties in order to participate in the planning and implementation of the campaign. However, all members of the administrative team must be kept abreast of all aspects of the campaign. This can be done through the regular administrative team newsletter. Also, the superintendent could begin the administrative team meetings with an update on the campaign. By keeping all administrators aware of the progress of the campaign, they, in turn, can share the information with their staffs.

Administrative team members can play an active role in the campaign and should urge their staffs to do the same. They can wear campaign lapel badges to indicate their support. Building administrators should have campaign materials on hand for parents and visitors to pick up. They should be prepared to answer questions and clarify issues from parents who visit or call on the telephone. If there are questions they cannot answer, they should refer them to either the campaign committee or to the central office.

The Teachers and Classified Staff

The campaign committee should have a representative from the teachers' association and from the classified staff. If possible, provision should be made for released time to allow them to participate in campaign planning and implementation. It also is important for all teachers and classified staff to be informed about what the campaign committee is doing so they will feel a part of the process and will share that information with friends and neighbors. However, teachers should avoid campaigning with students during their regular classes. This could be viewed as a form of indoctrination if the students go home and try to pressure parents into voting for the levy or bond issue.

The Students

It is easy to generate enthusiasm for the campaign among students because they most likely will be the beneficiaries of a successful campaign. However, their use in the campaign must be handled in ways that will not be viewed as exploitation. A student should be represented on the campaign committee. A mature young person can add a great deal to the planning and implementation of a campaign and learn a lot in the process. A committed staff member should serve as a liaison with students who volunteer to work on the campaign and help to coordinate their activities.

Students can write letters to the editor. If there is a student page in the local newspaper, they can write articles supporting the levy or bond and point out specific aspects that will benefit students. Often the poignancy of a student letter or article carries greater persuasive power than one from an adult. In addition to writing activities, students could organize a parade, pass out literature, wear sandwich boards around the community just prior to election day, participate in a windshield project, and record the campaign song.

The Architects

When a bond issue is intended for a new school, there will be lots of questions about the new structure. The best person to answer these questions is a representative of the architectural firm that designed the building. The availability of the architect at public meetings can be a great asset for the campaign committee.

Conclusion

Everyone associated with a successful campaign deserves a special thank you. And being a good winner means extending the olive branch to those who opposed the issue. This is no time to gloat or put them down. The support of these people next time around may be very important. You also are likely to hear from some persons who will claim that they voted for the levy or bond issue even though you're certain that they did not. Smile and thank them anyway. Likewise after a loss, the thank-you notes must flow. As hard as it might be, avoid pointing fingers or placing blame. Treat the loss as but one step in a long-range process of developing community support. Assess the factors that contributed to the loss and design strategies to address them in your next campaign.

Convert campaign enthusiasm into ongoing efforts for marketing other school programs. Keep the channels of communication with business and industry, the media, supporters and nonsupporters alike open and flowing. Strategies used in the campaign should become permanent public relations tools for the schools.

The marketing approach advocated in this fastback is more than just a few gimmicks to win a levy or bond issue. It is an approach that can serve school leaders in a host of ways. It starts with the marketing premise that "having what you can get rid of" is more important than "getting rid of what you have." It means having a firm grasp of those variables (economic, social, cultural, legal) that a market survey will reveal. It means having an understanding of how community demographics and other variables are related to "customer" satisfaction.

The time has come for school districts to adopt the marketing concepts of product, price, promotion, and distribution and to use them to maximize the overall satisfaction of their various constituencies.

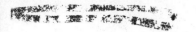

DEMCO